★★★★★

MLB TEAMS

Minnesota TWINS

KENNY ABDO

Fly!
An Imprint of Abdo Zoom
abdobooks.com

abdobooks.com

Published by Abdo Zoom, a division of ABDO, P.O. Box 398166, Minneapolis, Minnesota 55439.

Printed in the United States of America, North Mankato, Minnesota.
102025
012026

THIS BOOK CONTAINS RECYCLED MATERIALS

Photo Credits: AP Images, Getty Images, Icon Sportswire, Shutterstock
Production Contributors: Kenny Abdo, Jennie Forsberg, Grace Hansen
Design Contributors: Candice Keimig, Neil Klinepier

Library of Congress Control Number: 2025936775

Publisher's Cataloging-in-Publication Data

Names: Abdo, Kenny, author.
Title: Minnesota Twins / by Kenny Abdo
Description: Minneapolis, Minnesota : Abdo Zoom, 2026 | Series: MLB teams | Includes online resources and index.
Identifiers: ISBN 9798384940258 (lib. bdg.) | ISBN 9798384941019 (ebook) | ISBN 9798384941392 (read-to-me ebook)
Subjects: LCSH: Minnesota Twins (Baseball team)--Juvenile literature. | Baseball teams--Juvenile literature. | Professional sports--Juvenile literature. | Sports franchises--Juvenile literature. | Major League Baseball (Organization)--Juvenile literature.
Classification: DDC 796.357--dc23

Table of CONTENTS

Twins 4

Batter Up! 8

Grand Slams 14

Hall of Fame 24

Glossary 30

Online Resources 31

Index 32

TWINS

Since moving to the Twin Cities in 1961, the Minnesota Twins have doubled the excitement and fun!

CHW 301 000 0
MIN 000 100 0
THOME
25
twinsbaseball.com
Carrier
twinsbaseball.com
Carrier
Carrier

With multiple **American League (AL) pennants** and World Series titles, the Twins bring the heat to the chilly northern state!

BATTER UP!

The Minnesota Twins began in 1901 as the Washington Senators of Washington, DC. In 1961, the team moved west and got a new name. They became the Twins, a nod to the Twin Cities of Minneapolis and St. Paul.

Twins

In 1965, the Twins won the **AL pennant** and faced the Dodgers in the World Series. Tony Oliva led the offense, and Mudcat Grant pitched with power. The Twins lost in seven games, but the season is still a big highlight in the team's history.

In 1987, the Twins won their first World Series since moving to Minnesota! They faced the Cardinals and won in seven thrilling games. It was a huge moment for the team and its fans.

GRAND SLAMS

In 1991, the Twins became the first team to win the World Series after finishing last place the year before. In Game 6, Kirby Pucket hit a **walk-off** home run. The Twins went on to win it all in Game 7. It is still considered one of the greatest World Series ever played.

The 1990s were mostly tough for the Twins. The team began to rebuild with young players, working to return to the top. Fans gained hope after winning the **AL** Central **division** title in 2002, 2003, and 2004.

The Twins kept growing with young stars. Joe Mauer won three batting titles and the 2009 **AL** MVP Award. Torii Hunter earned several **Gold Gloves** for his defense. Both made multiple **All-Star** teams, proving the Twins had a strong pipeline of talent.

MAUER
7

The Twins made six playoff appearances between 2002 and 2010. They won the **AL** Central five times during that stretch. In 2006, Johan Santana earned the **Cy Young Award** and Justin Morneau won the AL MVP.

Twins
33
KENESAW MOUNTAIN LANDIS
MOST
VALUABLE PLAYER
AMERICAN LEAGUE
MEMORIAL BASEBALL AWARD
125
Louisville Slugger

MINNESOTA
49

In 2019, the Twins set an MLB single-season home run **record**. The team clinched the **AL** Central **Division** title in 2019, 2020, and 2023. Pablo López has been a dominant force for the Twins since 2023, though the pitcher struggled with injuries in 2025. The team and its fans hope the future looks bright.

HALL OF FAME

Harmon Killebrew was a power hitter for the Twins and one of the game's top sluggers. He hit 559 home runs and led the **AL** in homers six times. In 1969, Killebrew won the MVP Award and helped the Twins make the playoffs. He was named to the Baseball Hall of Fame in 1984.

Rod Carew played for the Twins from 1967 to 1978 and became one of baseball's best hitters. He won seven batting titles and earned the **AL** MVP Award in 1977. Carew made 12 **All-Star** teams with Minnesota and finished with a .334 batting average. He entered the Baseball Hall of Fame in 1991.

Twins

Kirby Puckett was a star player for the Twins from 1984 to 1995. He collected 2,304 hits, 207 home runs, and finished with a .318 batting average. Puckett made 10 **All-Star** teams and won six **Gold Gloves**. He helped lead the Twins to World Series titles in 1987 and 1991. Puckett was named to the Baseball Hall of Fame in 2001.

GLOSSARY

All-Star – consisting of athletes chosen as the best at their positions from all teams in a league or region.

American League (AL) – one of two 15-team leagues that make up MLB.

Cy Young Award – an annual American baseball award given to the best pitcher in each of the two MLB leagues.

division – a number of teams grouped together in a sport for competitive purposes.

Gold Glove Award – an annual award given to the best fielders at each position in both the AL and National League (NL).

pennant – the title achieved by the team that wins its division or league championship.

record – a top achievement by a player or team that no one has done before.

walk-off – any victory in which the home team scores the winning run in the bottom of the final inning.

Wild Card Series – the first round of the postseason.

ONLINE RESOURCES

Booklinks
NONFICTION NETWORK
FREE! ONLINE NONFICTION RESOURCES

To learn more about the Minnesota Twins, please visit **abdobooklinks.com** or scan this QR code. These links are routinely monitored and updated to provide the most current information available.

INDEX

awards 18, 20, 25, 26, 28
Cardinals (team) 13
Carew, Rod 26
championships 7, 13, 14, 28
Dodgers (team) 11
Grant, Mudcat 11
Hunter, Torii 18
Killebrew, Harmon 25
López, Pablo 23
Mauer, Joe 18
Minnesota 13
Morneau, Justin 20
Oliva, Tony 11
Puckett, Kirby 14, 28
records 23
Santana, Johan 20
Washington, DC 9